RESCUED! ANIMAL ES[…]

Mason
VERSUS THE
Tornado
DOG RESCUE!

BY JAMES BUCKLEY JR.

ILLUSTRATED BY KERSTIN LACROSS

BEARPORT
PUBLISHING

Minneapolis, Minnesota

BEAR
CLAW

Credits

Interior coloring by Jon Siruno.
Interior inks by Haley Boros.
Photos: 22T © Mark Schiefelebin/AP Photos; 22B © Sue Ogrocki/AP Photos.

Bearport Publishing
Minneapolis, MN
President: Jen Jenson
Director of Product Development: Spencer Brinker
Editor: Allison Juda

Produced by Shoreline Publishing Group LLC
Santa Barbara, California
Designer: Patty Kelley
Editorial Director: James Buckley Jr.

DISCLAIMER: This graphic story is a dramatization based on true events. It is intended to give the reader a sense of the narrative rather than a presentation of actual details as they occurred.

Library of Congress Cataloging-in-Publication Data

Names: Buckley, James, Jr., 1963- author.
Title: Mason versus the tornado : dog rescue! / by James Buckley Jr.
Description: Bear claw books edition. | Minneapolis, Minnesota : Bearport
   Publishing Company, [2021] | Series: Rescued! animal escapes | Includes
   bibliographical references and index.
Identifiers: LCCN 2020039087 (print) | LCCN 2020039088 (ebook) | ISBN
   9781647476182 (library binding) | ISBN 9781647476250 (paperback) | ISBN
   9781647476328 (ebook)
Subjects: LCSH: Dog rescue—Juvenile literature. | Tornadoes—Juvenile
   literature.
Classification: LCC HV4746 .B667 2021 (print) | LCC HV4746 (ebook) | DDC
   636.7/0832—dc23
LC record available at https://lccn.loc.gov/2020039087
LC ebook record available at https://lccn.loc.gov/2020039088

For more information, write to Bearport Publishing, 5357 Penn Avenue South, Minneapolis, MN 55419. Printed in the United States of America.

CONTENTS

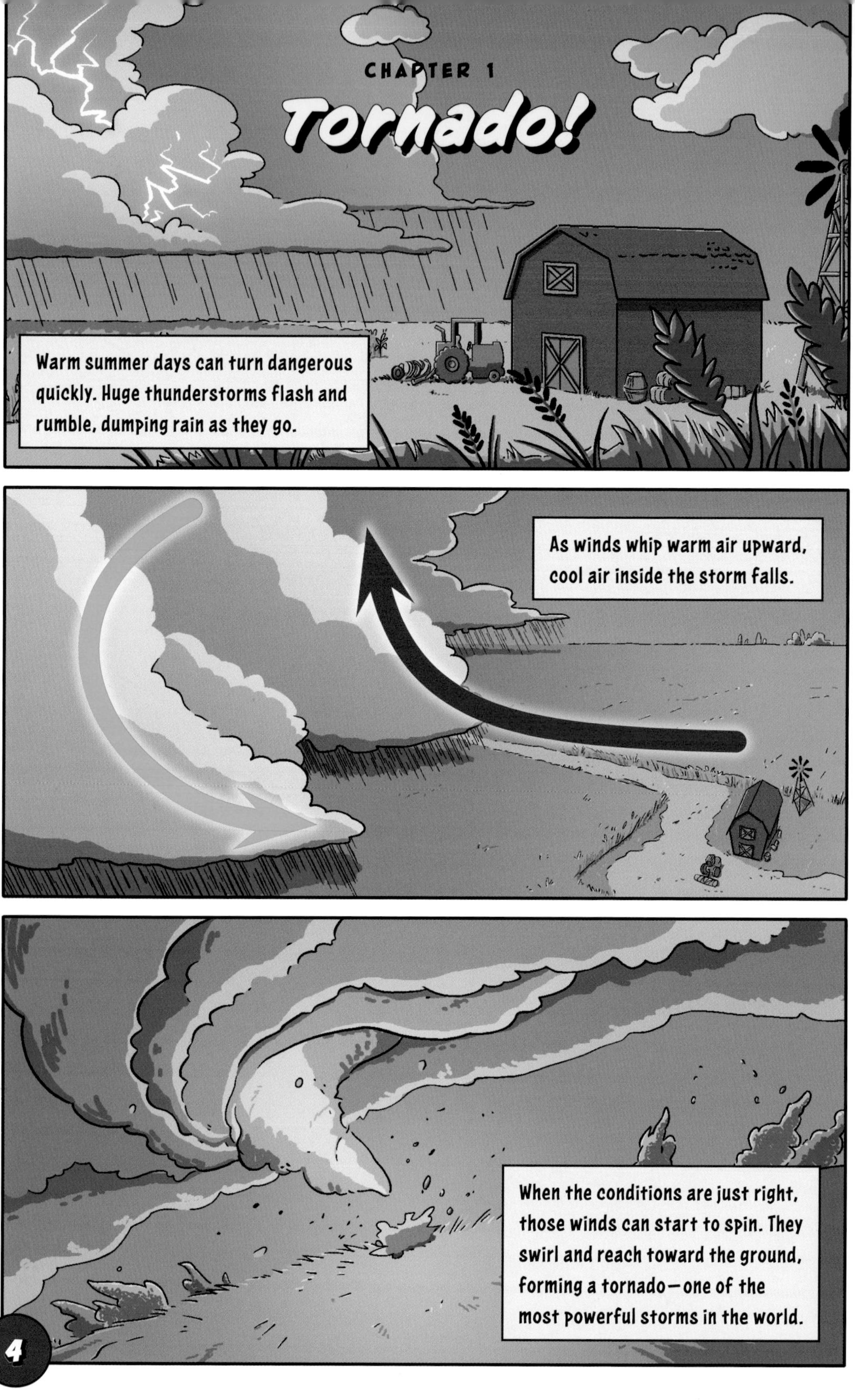
CHAPTER 1
Tornado!
Warm summer days can turn dangerous quickly. Huge thunderstorms flash and rumble, dumping rain as they go.
As winds whip warm air upward, cool air inside the storm falls.
When the conditions are just right, those winds can start to spin. They swirl and reach toward the ground, forming a tornado—one of the most powerful storms in the world.

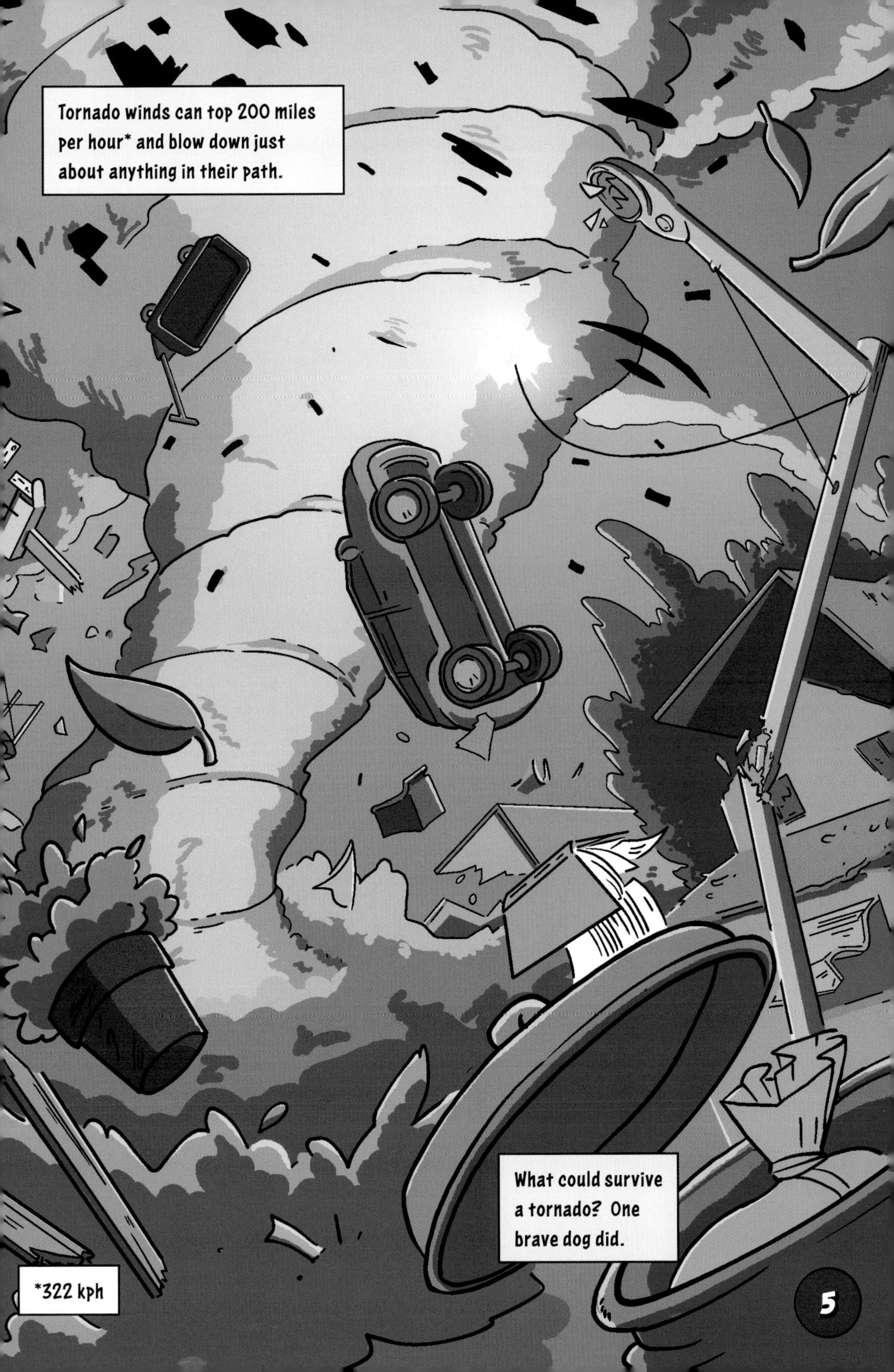
Tornado winds can top 200 miles per hour* and blow down just about anything in their path.
What could survive a tornado? One brave dog did.
*322 kph

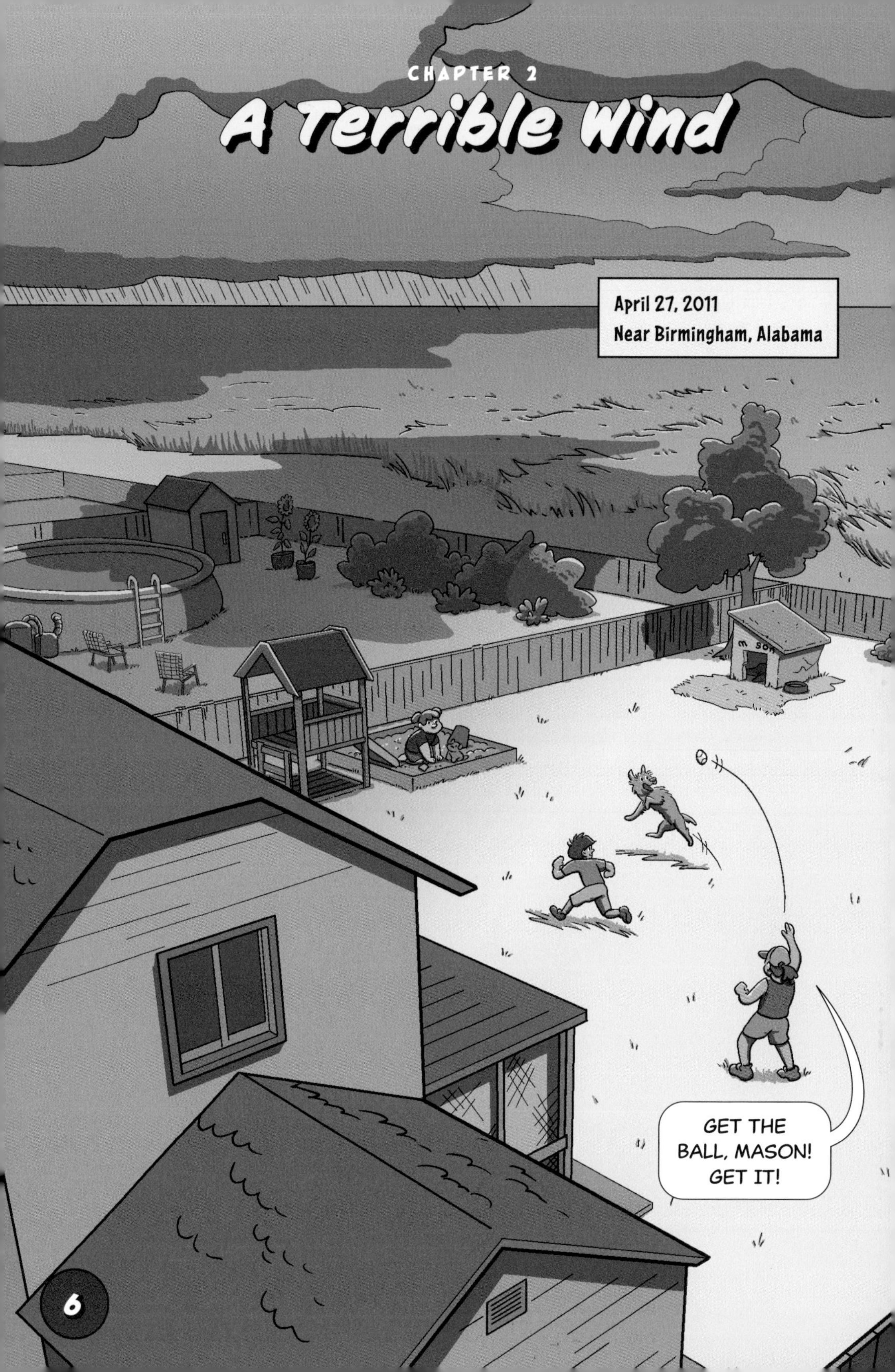
CHAPTER 2
A Terrible Wind
April 27, 2011
Near Birmingham, Alabama
GET THE BALL, MASON! GET IT!

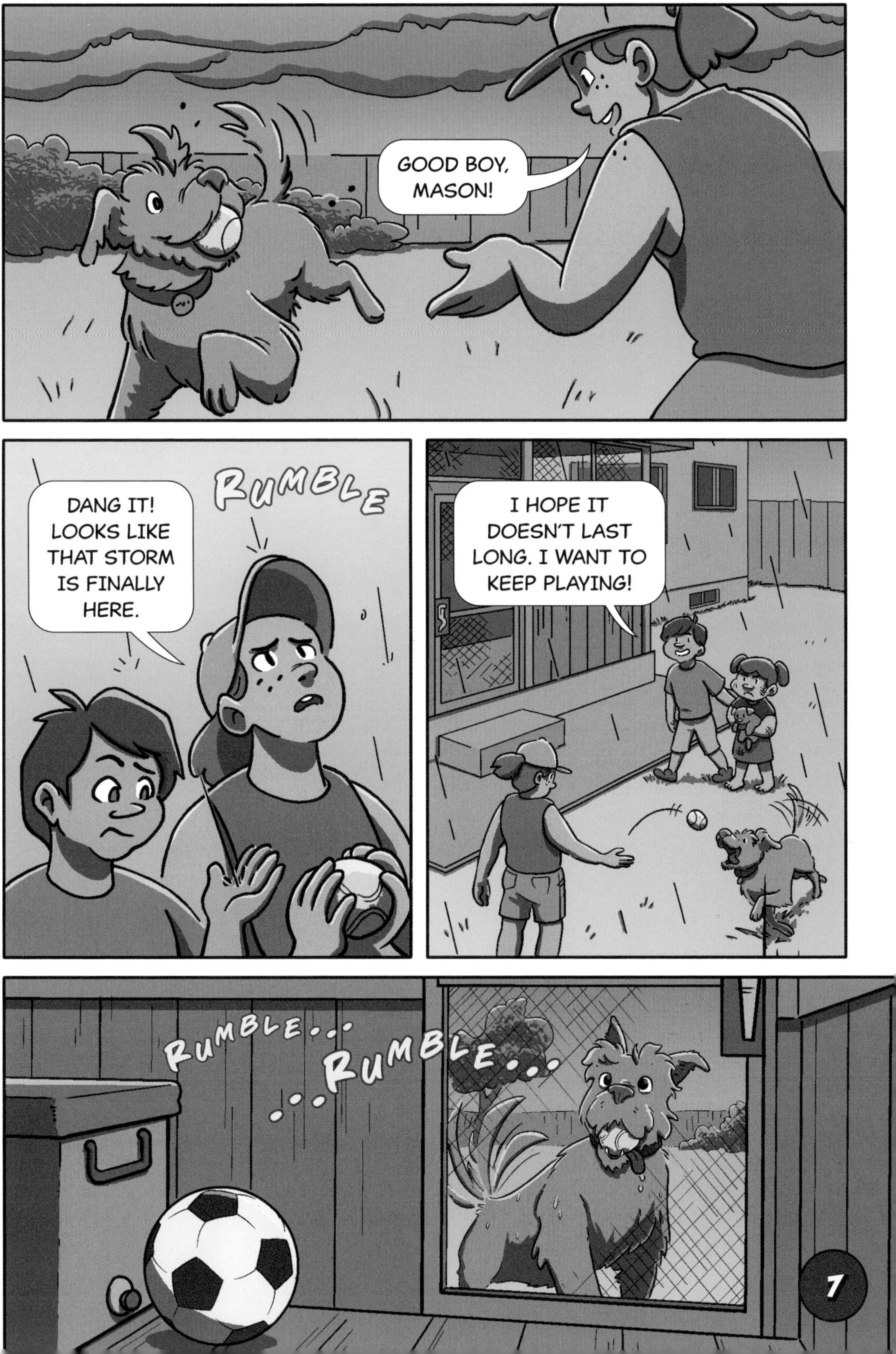
GOOD BOY, MASON!
DANG IT! LOOKS LIKE THAT STORM IS FINALLY HERE.
RUMBLE
I HOPE IT DOESN'T LAST LONG. I WANT TO KEEP PLAYING!
RUMBLE...
...RUMBLE...

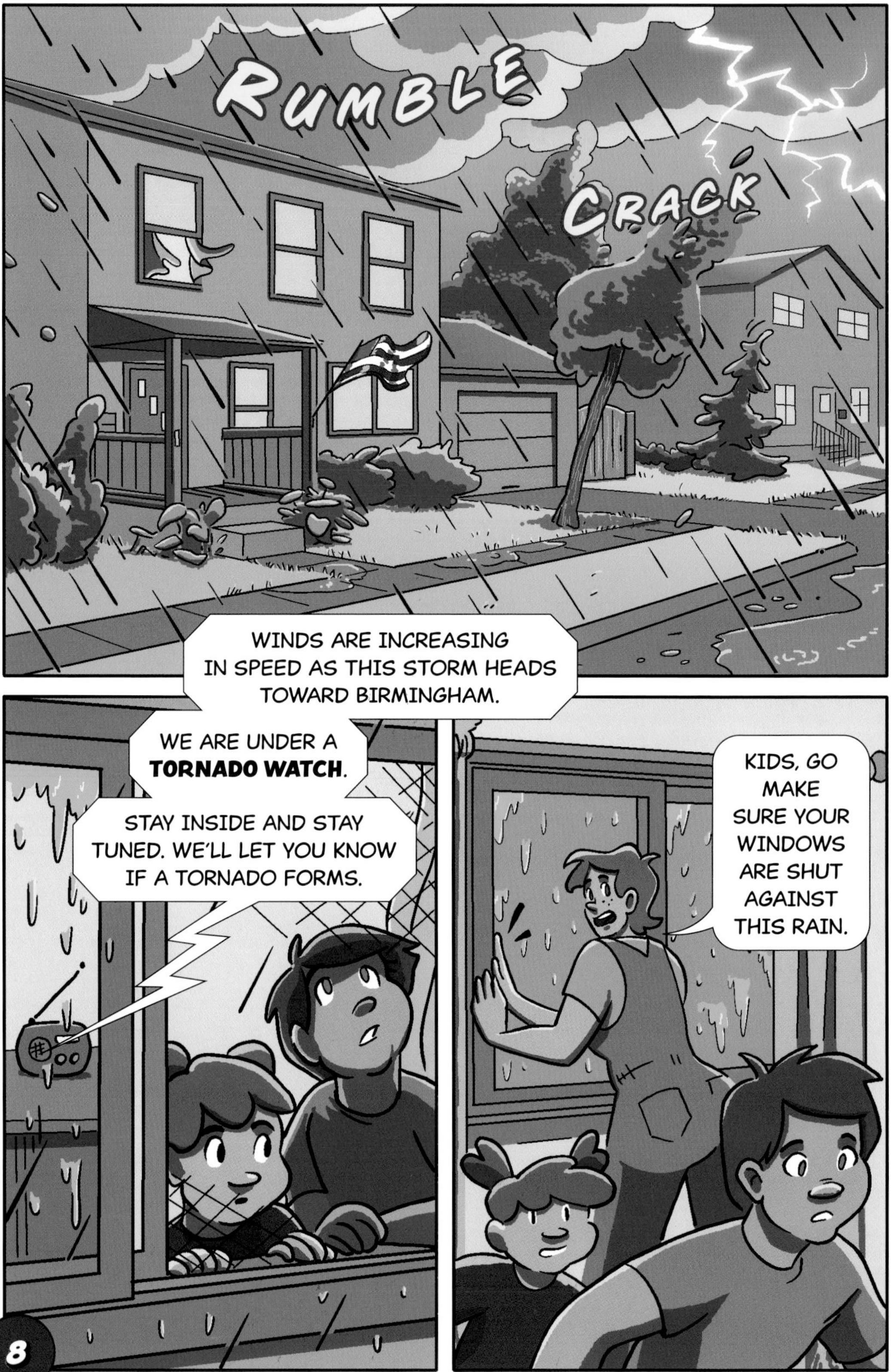
RUMBLE
CRACK
WINDS ARE INCREASING IN SPEED AS THIS STORM HEADS TOWARD BIRMINGHAM.
WE ARE UNDER A **TORNADO WATCH**.
STAY INSIDE AND STAY TUNED. WE'LL LET YOU KNOW IF A TORNADO FORMS.
KIDS, GO MAKE SURE YOUR WINDOWS ARE SHUT AGAINST THIS RAIN.

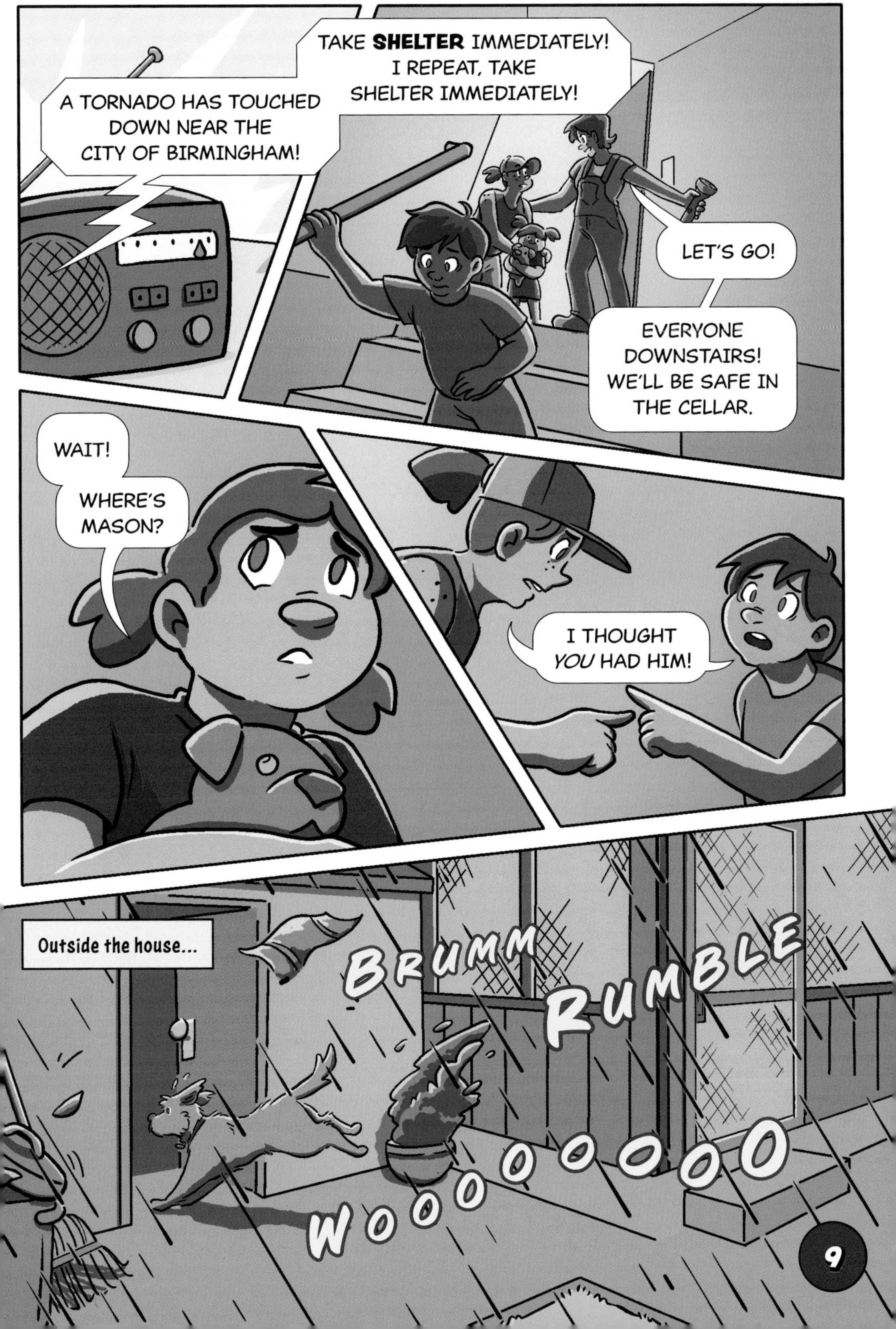
A TORNADO HAS TOUCHED DOWN NEAR THE CITY OF BIRMINGHAM!
TAKE **SHELTER** IMMEDIATELY! I REPEAT, TAKE SHELTER IMMEDIATELY!
LET'S GO!
EVERYONE DOWNSTAIRS! WE'LL BE SAFE IN THE CELLAR.
WAIT!
WHERE'S MASON?
I THOUGHT *YOU* HAD HIM!
Outside the house...
BRUMM
RUMBLE
WOOOOOOOOO

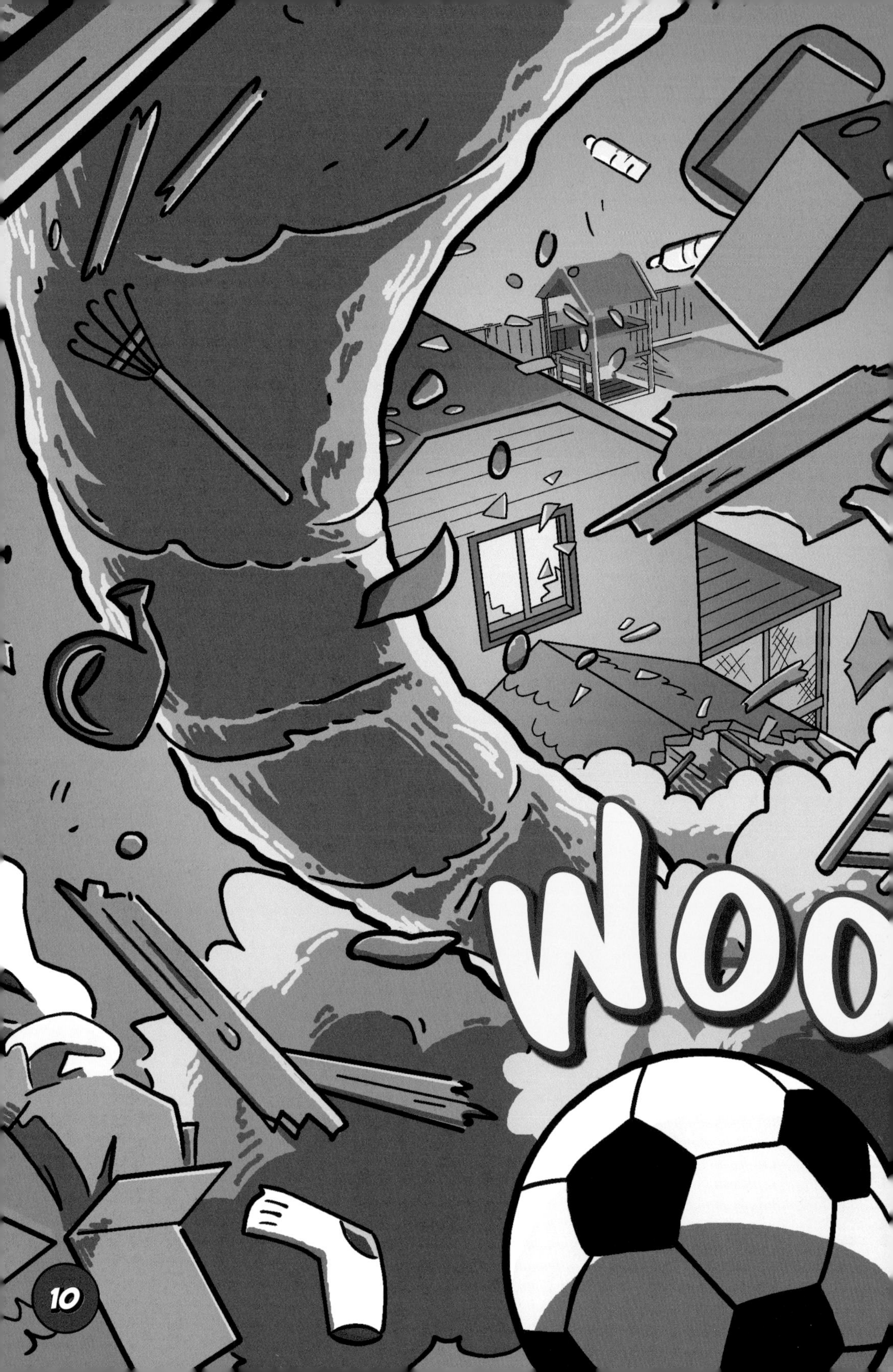
WOO

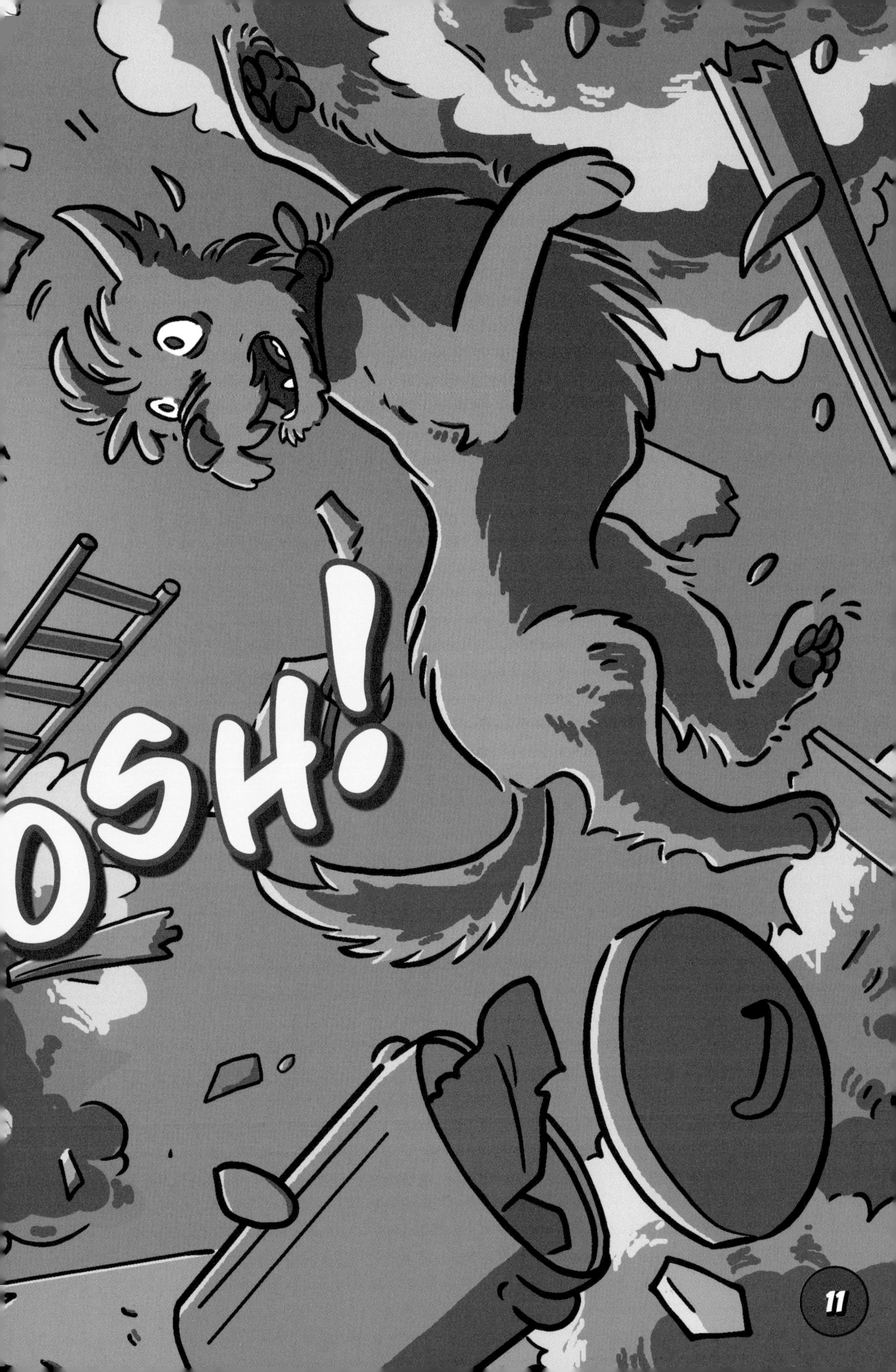
OSH!

CHAPTER 3

The Search for Mason

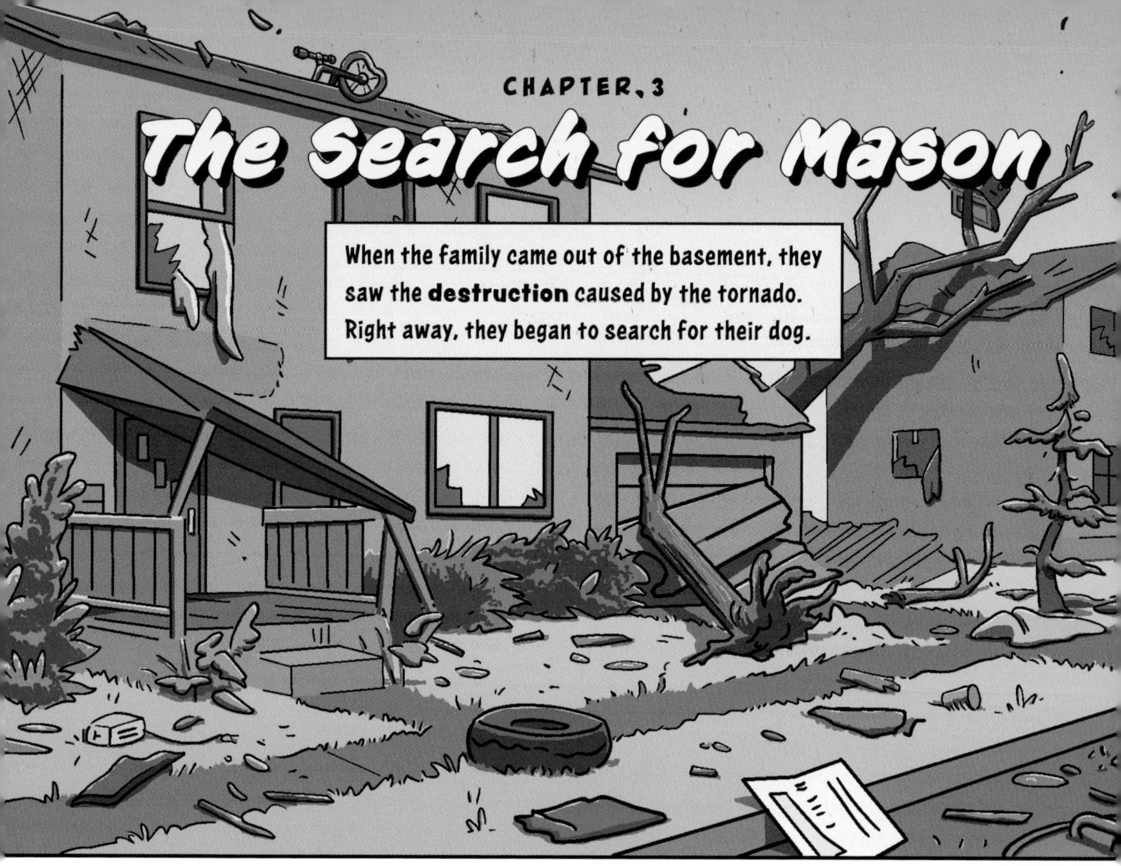
When the family came out of the basement, they saw the **destruction** caused by the tornado. Right away, they began to search for their dog.

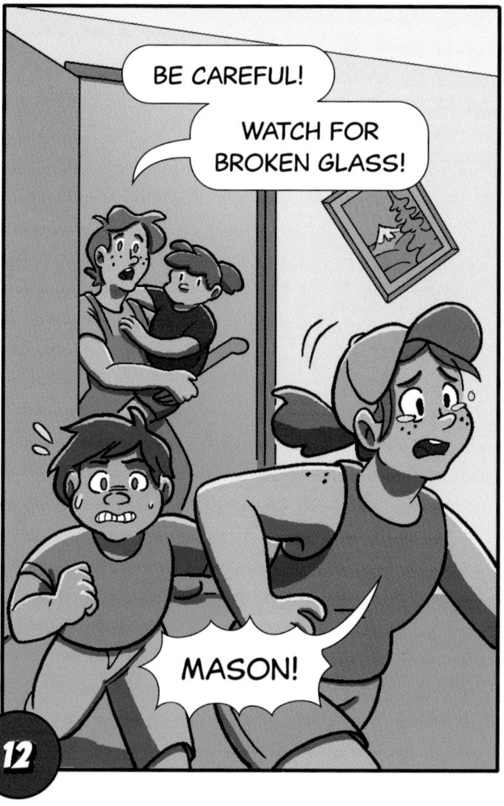
BE CAREFUL!
WATCH FOR BROKEN GLASS!
MASON!

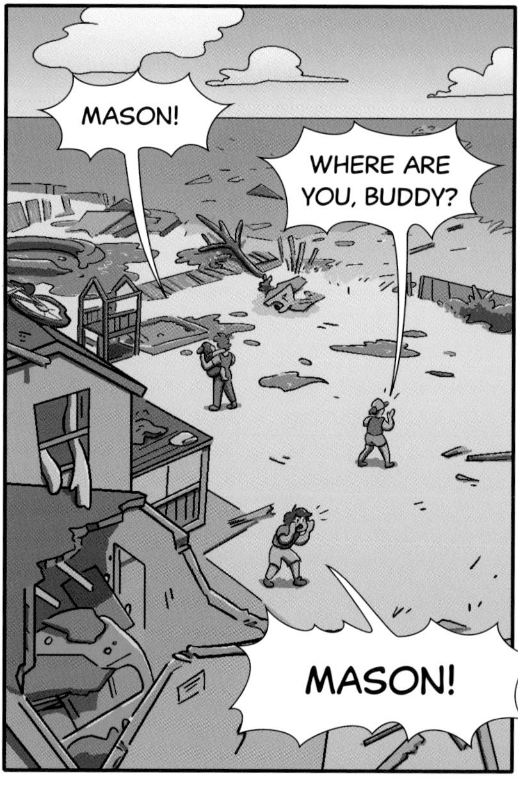
MASON!
WHERE ARE YOU, BUDDY?
MASON!

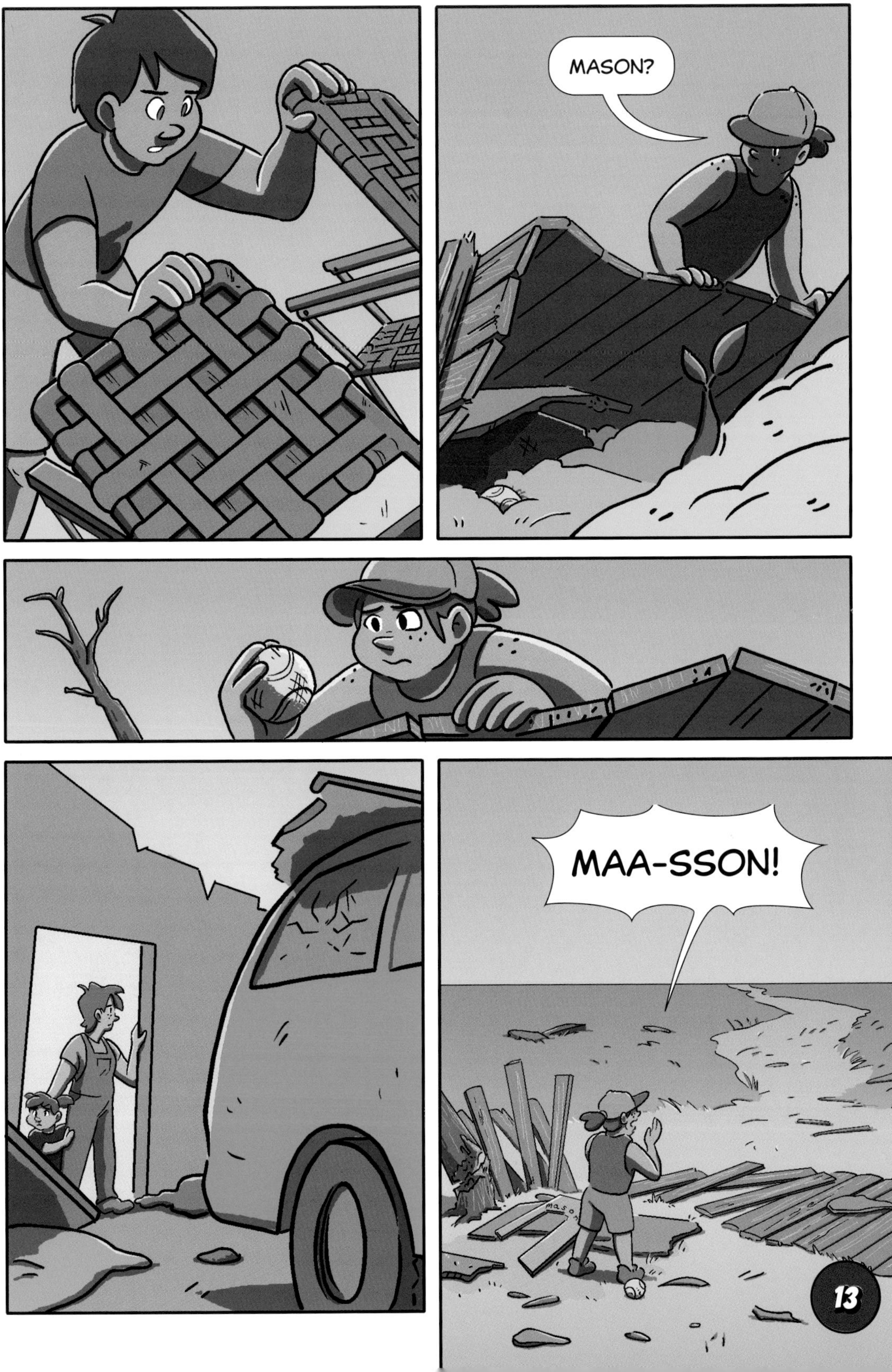
MASON?
MAA-SSON!

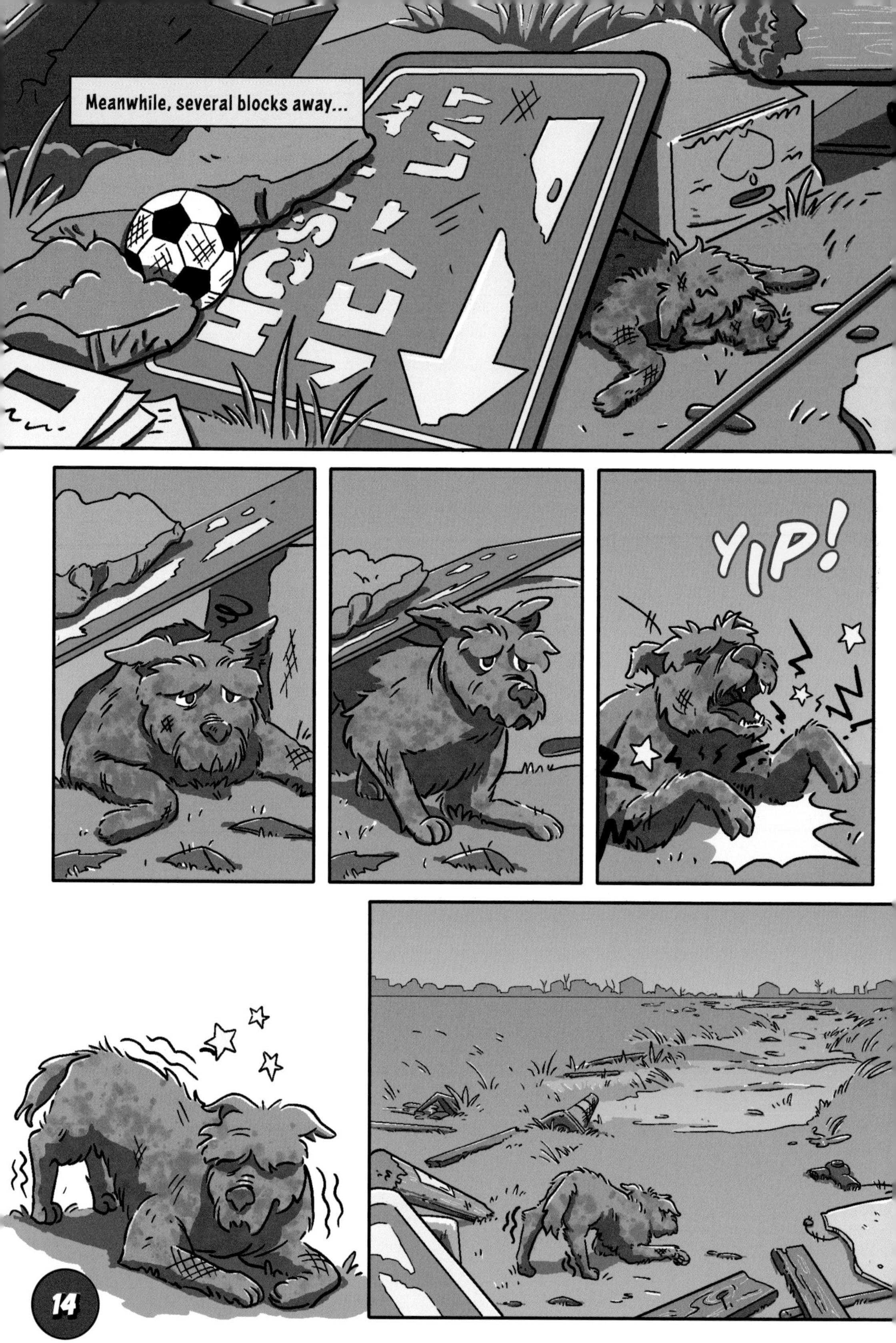

Meanwhile, several blocks away...
YIP!

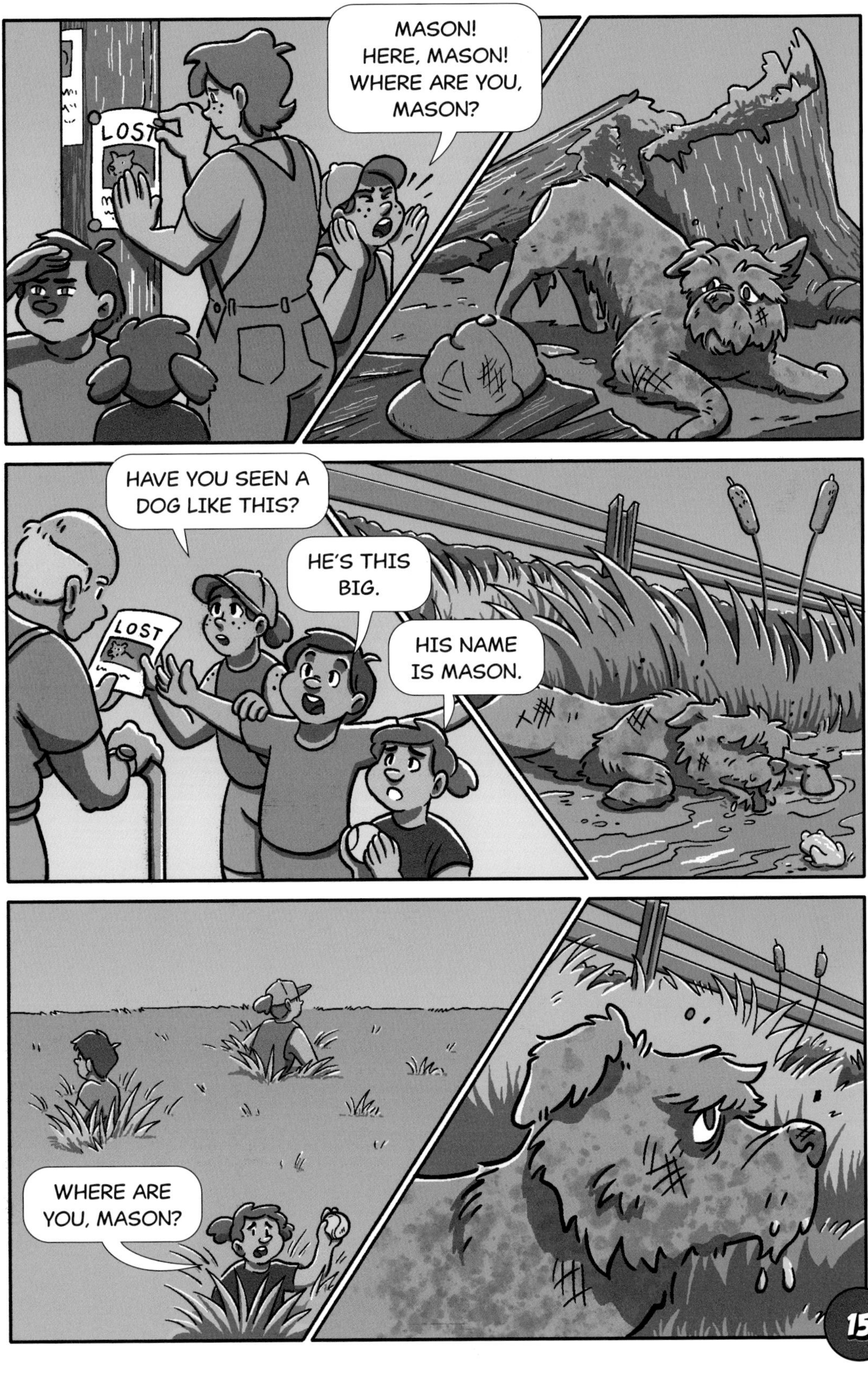
LOST
MASON! HERE, MASON! WHERE ARE YOU, MASON?
HAVE YOU SEEN A DOG LIKE THIS?
LOST
HE'S THIS BIG.
HIS NAME IS MASON.
WHERE ARE YOU, MASON?

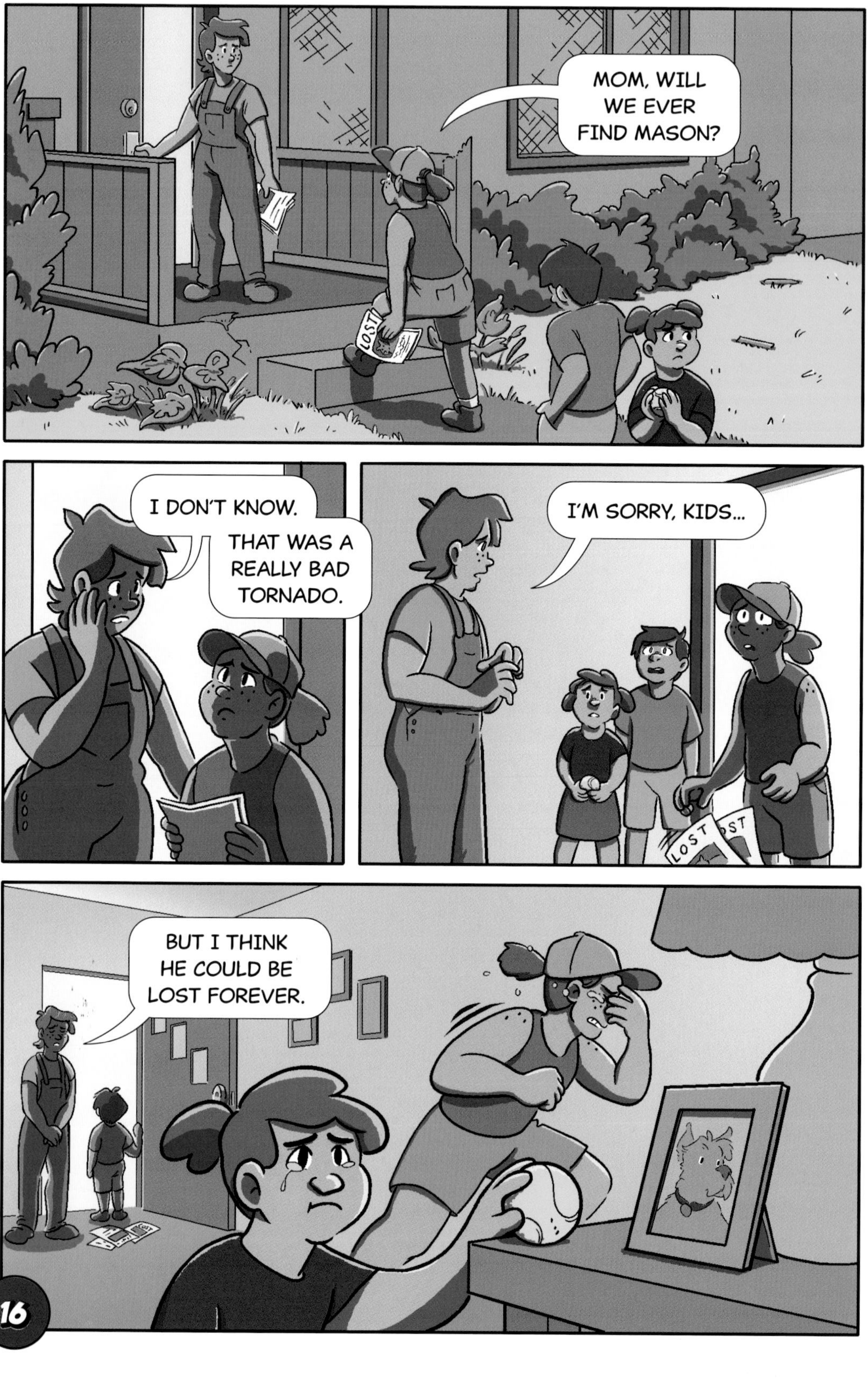
MOM, WILL WE EVER FIND MASON?
LOST
I DON'T KNOW.
THAT WAS A REALLY BAD TORNADO.
I'M SORRY, KIDS...
LOST
BUT I THINK HE COULD BE LOST FOREVER.

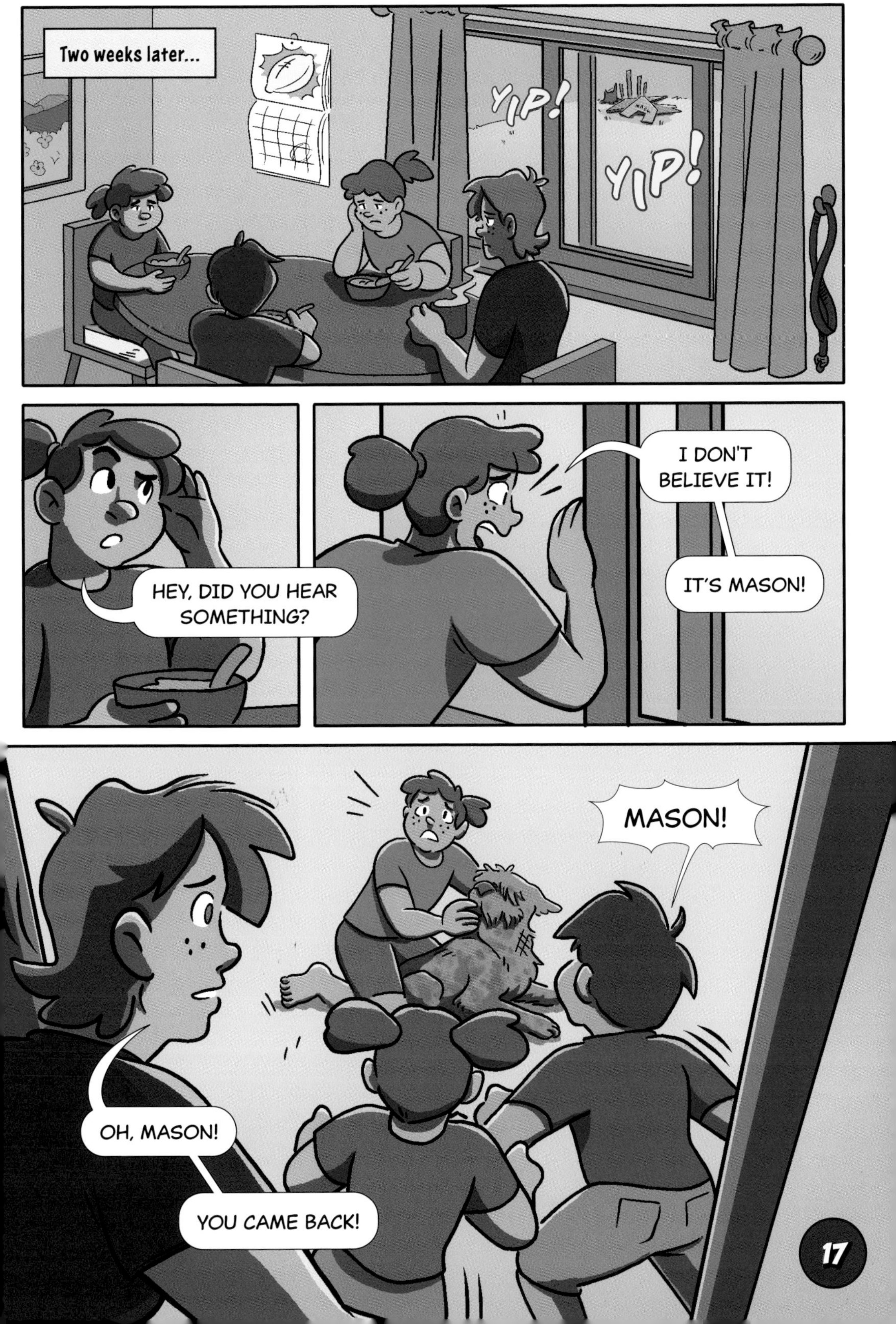
Two weeks later...
YIP!
YIP!
HEY, DID YOU HEAR SOMETHING?
I DON'T BELIEVE IT!
IT'S MASON!
MASON!
OH, MASON!
YOU CAME BACK!

CHAPTER 4

An Incredible Comeback

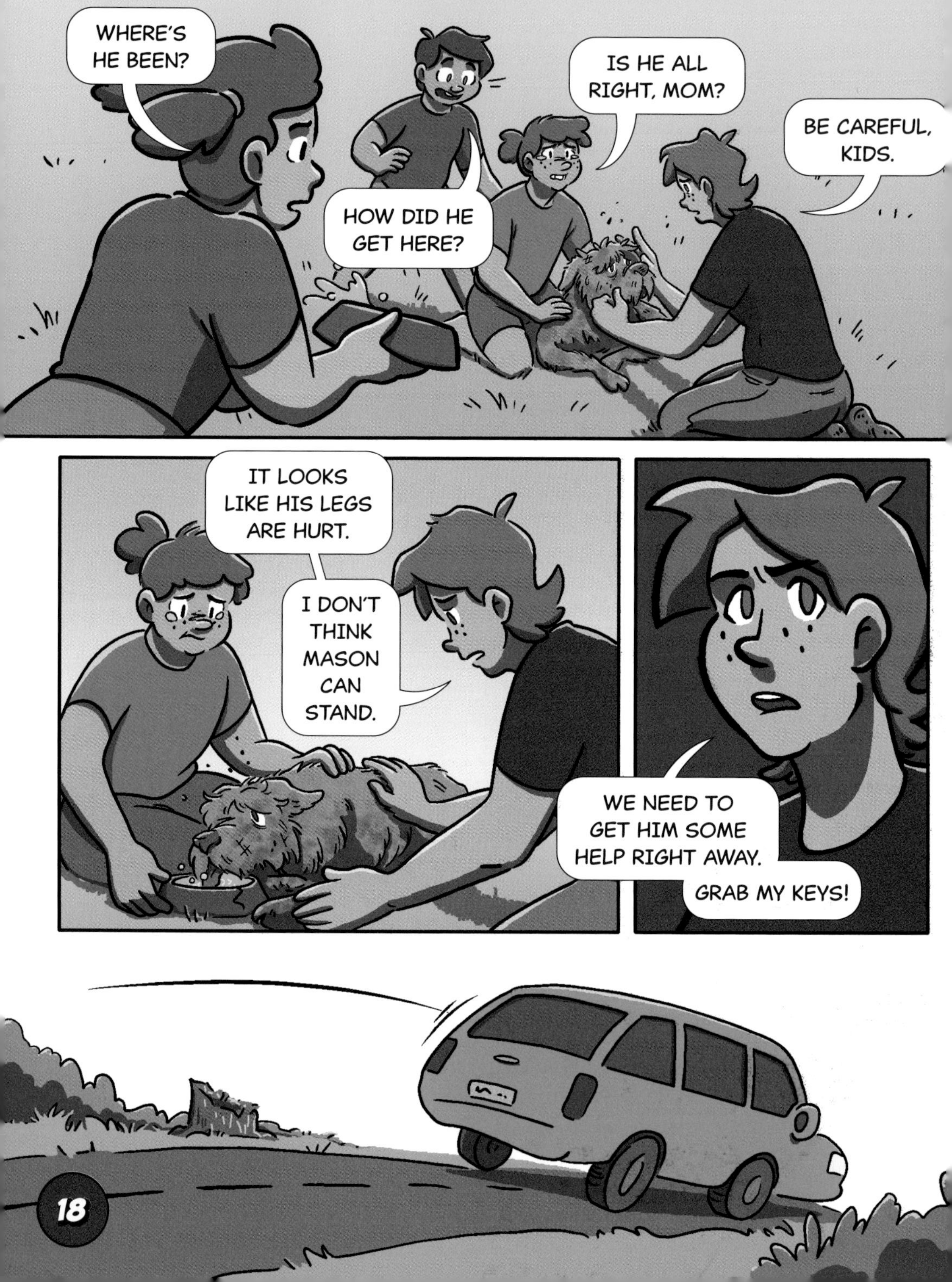
WHERE'S HE BEEN?
HOW DID HE GET HERE?
IS HE ALL RIGHT, MOM?
BE CAREFUL, KIDS.
IT LOOKS LIKE HIS LEGS ARE HURT.
I DON'T THINK MASON CAN STAND.
WE NEED TO GET HIM SOME HELP RIGHT AWAY.
GRAB MY KEYS!

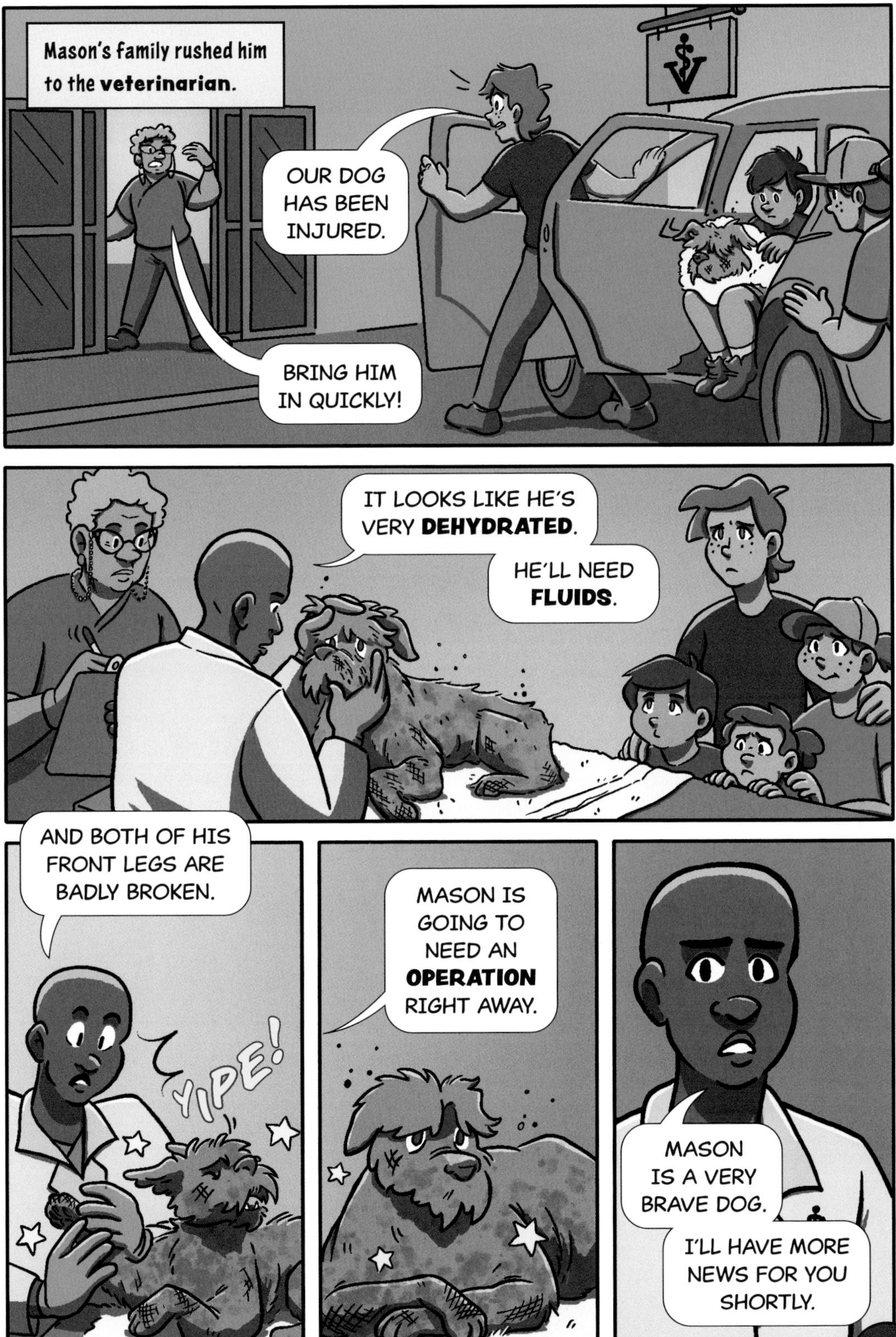
Mason's family rushed him to the **veterinarian.**
OUR DOG HAS BEEN INJURED.
BRING HIM IN QUICKLY!
IT LOOKS LIKE HE'S VERY **DEHYDRATED**.
HE'LL NEED **FLUIDS**.
AND BOTH OF HIS FRONT LEGS ARE BADLY BROKEN.
YIPE!
MASON IS GOING TO NEED AN **OPERATION** RIGHT AWAY.
MASON IS A VERY BRAVE DOG.
I'LL HAVE MORE NEWS FOR YOU SHORTLY.

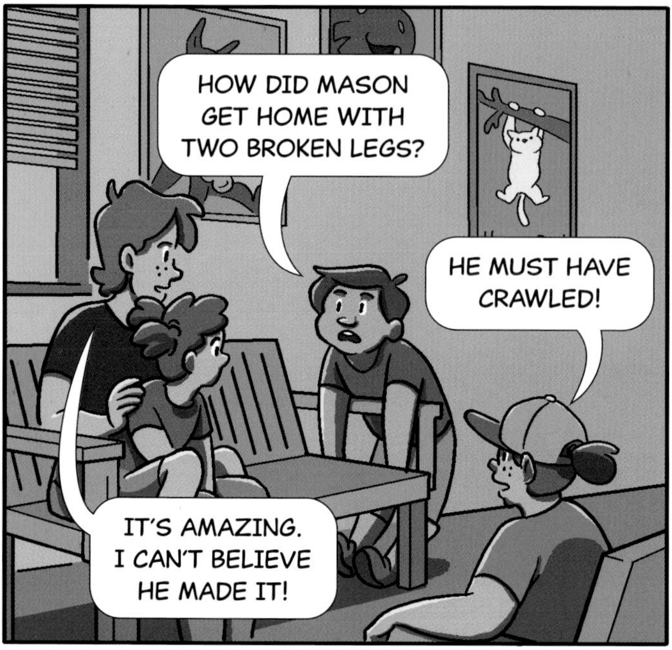
HOW DID MASON GET HOME WITH TWO BROKEN LEGS?
HE MUST HAVE CRAWLED!
IT'S AMAZING. I CAN'T BELIEVE HE MADE IT!
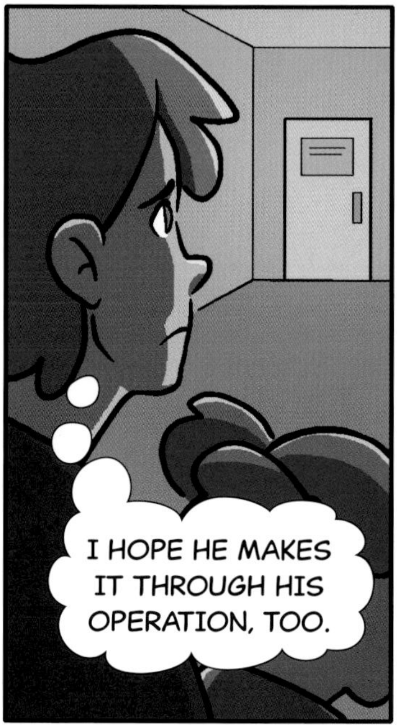
I HOPE HE MAKES IT THROUGH HIS OPERATION, TOO.
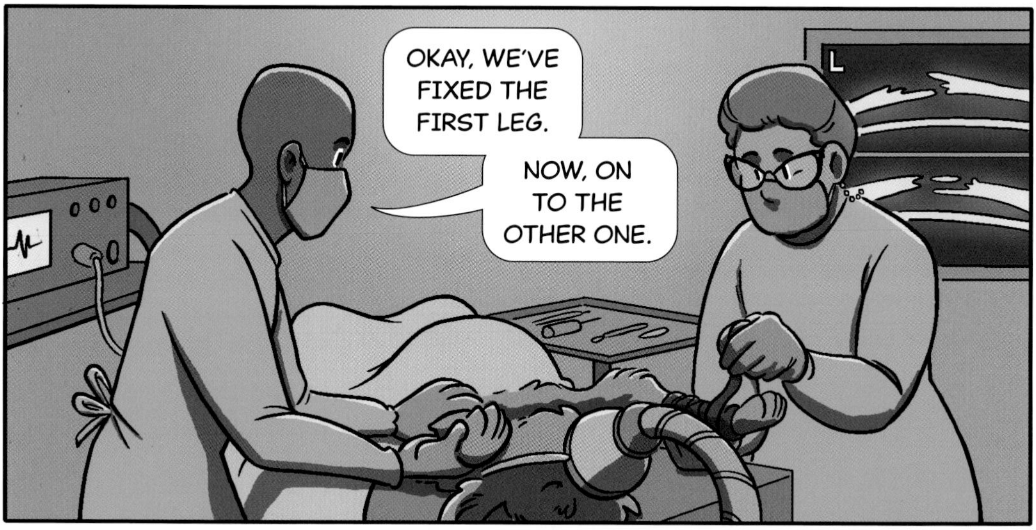
OKAY, WE'VE FIXED THE FIRST LEG.
NOW, ON TO THE OTHER ONE.
L
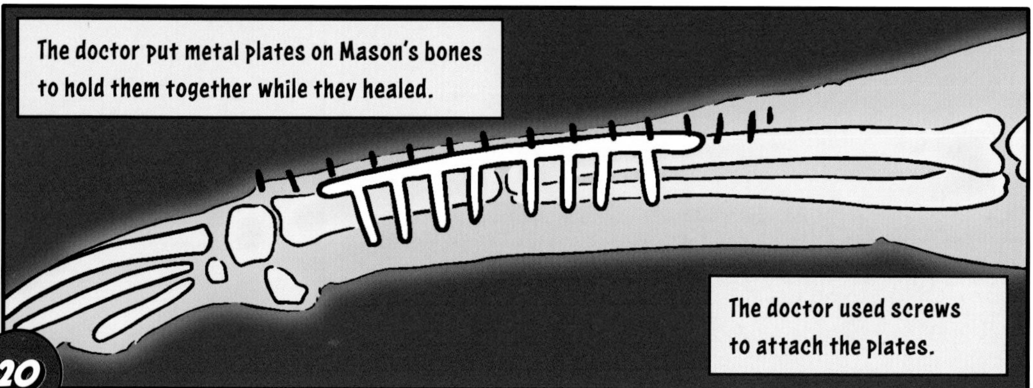
The doctor put metal plates on Mason's bones to hold them together while they healed.
The doctor used screws to attach the plates.

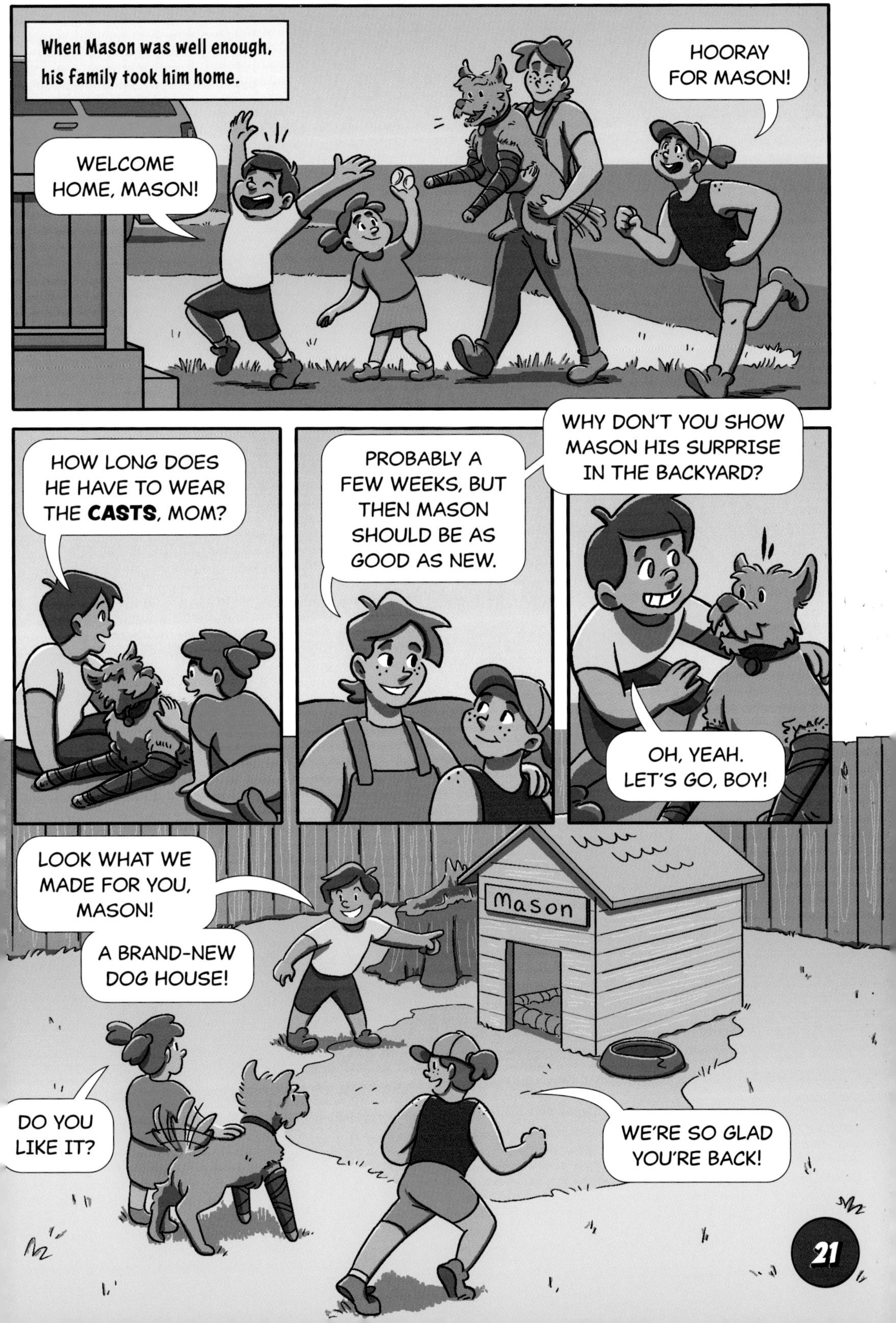
When Mason was well enough, his family took him home.
WELCOME HOME, MASON!
HOORAY FOR MASON!
HOW LONG DOES HE HAVE TO WEAR THE **CASTS**, MOM?
PROBABLY A FEW WEEKS, BUT THEN MASON SHOULD BE AS GOOD AS NEW.
WHY DON'T YOU SHOW MASON HIS SURPRISE IN THE BACKYARD?
OH, YEAH. LET'S GO, BOY!
LOOK WHAT WE MADE FOR YOU, MASON!
A BRAND-NEW DOG HOUSE!
Mason
DO YOU LIKE IT?
WE'RE SO GLAD YOU'RE BACK!

OTHER
TORNADO RESCUES

GUTHRIE, OKLAHOMA
MAY 24, 2011

When five tornadoes roared through the small town of Guthrie, one of the buildings hit was the Guthrie Animal Shelter. More than 60 cats and dogs were in the building when the storm blew through. Amazingly, they all survived—even though the building was destroyed. Members of the Animal Rescue **Corps** rushed to Guthrie to help. They gathered the cats and dogs and drove them to animal shelters that had not been damaged by the tornadoes.

OKLAHOMA-KANSAS OUTBREAK
MAY 3, 1999

A total of 74 tornadoes hit Oklahoma and Kansas in one day, killing 46 people and damaging thousands of buildings. Many horses were injured in the storm. A veterinarian treated the horses, and **volunteers** helped by feeding the horses and cleaning their **stalls**. Rescuers with the Oklahoma City Animal Shelter took in lost pets and gave them medical care.

GLOSSARY

casts hard shells placed over broken limbs to protect them while they heal

corps a group of people doing a job together

dehydrated sick from not having enough water

destruction large amounts of damage over a wide area

fluids liquids

operation a medical procedure where a doctor cuts into a patient in order to help fix something

shelter a place where a person or animal is protected

stalls enclosed inside shelters for animals, usually horses

tornado watch an alert for when weather conditions are such that a tornado might form

veterinarian a doctor that cares for animals

volunteers people who work without pay

INDEX

READ MORE

Alderman, Christine Thomas. *Tornadoes (Bolt. Natural Disasters).* Mankato, MN: Black Rabbit Books, 2021.

Levy, Janey. *Devastating Storms (Mother Nature Is Trying to Kill Me!).* New York: Gareth Stevens, 2020.

Ventura, Marne. *Tornadoes (Surviving).* New York: Weigl, 2019.

LEARN MORE ONLINE

1. Go to **www.factsurfer.com**

2. Enter "**Mason vs Tornado**" into the search box.

3. Click on the cover of this book to see a list of websites.